Vietnam War POWs

by Danielle Smith-Llera

Content Adviser: Marc Leepson,
Vietnam Veterans of America,
Silver Spring, Maryland

Reading Adviser: Rosemary Palmer, Ph.D.,
Department of Literacy, College of Education,
Boise State University

Compass Point Books ✦ Minneapolis, Minnesota

Compass Point Books
151 Good Counsel Drive
P.O. Box 669
Mankato, MN 56002-0669

This book was manufactured with paper containing at least 10 percent post-consumer waste.

On the cover: Major Pewey Waddell was guarded by a militiawoman with a gun and bayonet after being captured in 1967.

Photographs ©: Billhardt/ullstein bild/The Granger Collection, New York, cover; Prints Old and Rare, back cover (far left); Library of Congress, back cover, 32; Bettmann/Corbis, 4, 13, 16, 19, 23, 31, 37, 40; Hulton Archive/Getty Images, 6, 8; Getty Images, 10; JP Laffont/Sygma/Corbis, 15; U.S. Air Force/Time Life Pictures/Getty Images, 17; DVIC/NARA, 21, 38; AP Images, 22; Archiv Gerstenberg/ullstein bild/The Granger Collection, New York, 25; Agence France Presse/Getty Images, 27; Bill Ray/Life Magazine/Time & Life Pictures/Getty Images, 29; AP Images/Richard Vogel, 33; Andrew Holbrooke/Corbis, 35.

Editor: Julie Gassman
Art Director/Page Production: LuAnn Ascheman-Adams
Photo Researcher: Eric Gohl
Cartographer: XNR Productions, Inc.
Library Consultant: Kathleen Baxter

Creative Director: Keith Griffin
Editorial Director: Nick Healy
Managing Editor: Catherine Neitge

Library of Congress Cataloging-in-Publication Data
Smith-Llera, Danielle, 1971–
   Vietnam War POWs / by Danielle Smith-Llera.
      p. cm. — (We the people)
   Includes index.
   ISBN 978-0-7565-3846-0 (library binding)
1. Vietnam War, 1961–1975—Prisoners and prisons, North Vietnamese—Juvenile literature. 2. Prisoners of war—United States—Juvenile literature.
3. Prisoners of war—Vietnam—Juvenile literature. I. Title. II. Series.
   DS559.4.S65 2008
   959.704'37—dc22   2008005736

Visit Compass Point Books on the Internet at *www.compasspointbooks.com*
or e-mail your request to *custserv@compasspointbooks.com*

TABLE OF CONTENTS

FROM PILOT TO PRISONER

Navy Lieutenant Commander Eugene McDaniel felt confident. He was soaring with a squadron of warplanes over North Vietnam on May 19, 1967. Suddenly a red light flashed on his control panel. A missile was coming toward his plane. A powerful blast followed. His control stick locked, and the plane rushed downward. McDaniel ejected from the plane in a "sickening kind of floating somersault." He struggled with his parachute, watching

Eugene McDaniel flew an A-6 Intruder during his last mission over North Vietnam.

the "jungle come rushing up." The North Vietnamese soldiers below watched his parachute float down into the trees. They captured him, removed his flight suit, and dressed him in Vietnamese clothes. Then McDaniel, like many other pilots, became a prisoner of war, a POW.

Beginning in 1965, American ground troops fought the North Vietnamese Army and the Viet Cong in South Vietnam's jungles. The Viet Cong were soldiers in South Vietnam who supported the efforts of North Vietnam but were not part of the regular army.

Also in 1965, American pilots began bombing North Vietnam heavily. These pilots made up most of the American POWs in North Vietnam. Other Americans, mostly ground troops, were captured by the Viet Cong and became POWs in the South. The approximately 690 American POWs held in both North and South Vietnam suffered, but their lives in prison were very different. Meanwhile, the Americans and the South Vietnamese captured their own prisoners.

North Vietnamese women and girls were active in many parts of the war, including the taking of prisoners.

The world watched how both sides in the Vietnam War treated their prisoners of war. The 35,000 prisoners held by the Americans and the South Vietnamese lived in decent conditions for the most part. But POWs held by the North Vietnamese and the Viet Cong suffered up to nine years of brutal treatment. Their imprisonment was the longest in U.S. history. Some POWs died. Others were never found. Those who lived say their fellow POWs helped them survive. Their families back home also helped by working for their release.

About the War

The Vietnam War was fought from 1959 to 1975. South Vietnam battled the communist Viet Cong of the South and the communists of North Vietnam. (Communists believe in an economic system in which goods and property are owned by the government and shared in common. Communist rulers limit personal freedoms to achieve their goals.)

The Viet Cong and the North Vietnamese wanted to unite the two countries into one communist nation. They were backed by the Soviet Union and China. The United States supported the South Vietnamese with money and troops. The first American combat troops arrived in 1965. By 1967, there were more than 500,000 U.S. troops fighting in Vietnam.

The fighting grew costly in lives and money. Protests against the war increased. In 1973, a cease-fire agreement was reached, and U.S. troops were withdrawn. Fighting continued, however, until 1975, when the North took control of a united Vietnam.

The war killed more than 58,000 Americans and between 2 million and 4 million Vietnamese. More than 300,000 Americans were wounded during the war, the longest in U.S. history. The effects of the long, bloody war are still felt today.

PIRATES OR POWs?

How prisoners were treated often depended on where they were captured. Some Americans captured in North Vietnam were marched on rope leashes. They were taken to prison camps with names such as Bang Liet, Xom Ap Lo,

Prisoners were sometimes paraded past the North Vietnamese people following their capture.

Loung Lang, Noi Coc, and Cu Loc. Not knowing the official names, the American POWs gave these camps nicknames: Skid Row, Briarpatch, Dogpatch, Rockpile, and Zoo. The nicknames reflected the conditions of the various prisons.

Navy Commander Howard Rutledge said these camps had windowless cells "not big enough for animals." Each filthy cell contained a bucket for a toilet and a slab of wood or cement for a bed, with shackles attached. More than 450 POWs suffered in camps throughout North Vietnam. Many were within 20 miles (32 kilometers) of the country's capital city, Hanoi. During scorching summers, guards would not let POWs bathe for months. During freezing winters without heat, the prisoners exercised to stay warm.

The prisoners' meals were often watery soup and pieces of bread filled with rat droppings. Rutledge described their drinking water as "thick with sewage, alive with para-sites." Rats ran over their food and bodies at night.

The prisoners were starving and often sick, and many lost weight. Some weighed as little as 100 pounds (45 kilograms) at the time of their release. Their captors rarely gave them medical care. Prisoners had to wrap each other's wounds, set broken bones, and even pull out rotten teeth.

Yet some POWs held in North Vietnam say that the American POWs held by the Viet Cong in South Vietnam

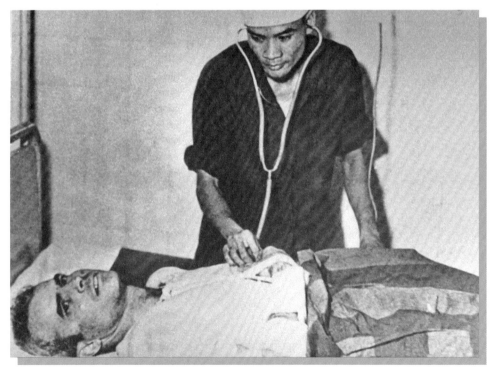

Lieutenant Commander John McCain, one of the most famous POWs, nearly died from his injuries.

Most of North Vietnam's prison camps were located near Hanoi, while those in South Vietnam were more spread out.

suffered more. These prisoners were often young soldiers.

Most did not have the survival training that the pilots

imprisoned in North Vietnam had. Life was horrible for

11

the approximately 200 POWs. They were not in permanent camps. Guards forced them to march through the jungle constantly. They were often kept in bamboo cages that also held leeches and cobras. Mosquitoes gave them malaria. Tight shackles numbed their limbs. The tropical sun burned them, or the heavy rains soaked them. The guards often kept them alone, sometimes for years. They starved, and many died. In addition, about 40 American soldiers were held in Cambodia, China, and Laos.

Only 30 POWs ever successfully escaped any of these camps. Escaping was difficult, mainly because the jungle was dangerous. Also, the prisoners were well-guarded and weak. Because they looked different from the country's native people, the Viet Cong could easily find them.

The POWs' minds suffered no matter where they were. It was difficult to spend days, months, and years with nothing to do. Air Force Colonel Theodore Guy, a former POW, said that "boredom and inactivity could prove as deadly as a bullet."

Why did the North Vietnamese and Viet Cong treat their POWs so badly? In 1949, North Vietnam, the United States, and other countries signed the International Conventions for the Protection of the Victims of War, known as the third Geneva Convention. This agreement explains how governments should treat captured military personnel. It says POWs should have clean rooms and healthy meals. It also says they should be allowed to gather

The third Geneva Convention stated that prisoners should be allowed to notify their next of kin about their capture.

13

with other prisoners and write letters home. However, North Vietnam did not believe their U.S. prisoners deserved this treatment. The United States bombed North Vietnam without formally declaring war. As a result, North Vietnam considered its prisoners "pirates."

The South Vietnamese held Viet Cong prisoners captured by U.S. troops. In some cases, the South Vietnamese did not treat their Viet Cong prisoners well. But the Americans tried to convince them to protect their POWs. The U.S. government hoped that if the Viet Cong prisoners were treated well, then the North Vietnamese would treat their American prisoners well.

In 1966, U.S. diplomat W. Averell Harriman ordered new prisons built in Bien Hoa, Da Nang, and other cities. Over the next five years, six camps were built throughout South Vietnam. They eventually held more than 35,000 prisoners. The prisoners got medical attention and were allowed visits from their families. They also received reading and writing lessons and were allowed to work for

U.S. officials visited the South Vietnamese prisons regularly in order to ensure that prisoners were treated well.

money. The United States gave sick or wounded prisoners the chance to return to their homes. However, many refused because they were treated so well in the camps.

Also in 1966, the International Committee of the Red Cross toured these camps holding Viet Cong prisoners. The committee praised the United States and South Vietnam for going "far beyond the requirements of the Geneva Convention." Yet North Vietnam did not let the Red Cross visit its camps. Therefore, the world did not know what was happening to the American POWs.

15

LIVING UNDER TORTURE

Navy Lieutenant Junior Grade Everett Alvarez Jr. remembered his torture: "All I could do was yell and scream to ride with the pain. ... Together they worked me over heartlessly, like a couple of kids pulling wings off flies."

A prisoner for more than eight years, Everett Alvarez Jr. was held longer than any other prisoner in North Vietnam.

The Hanoi Hilton was built in 1904, when Vietnam was under French rule.
The French built the prison to hold Vietnamese political prisoners.

Most often torture took place inside the North
Vietnamese prison named Hoa Lo. This camp held more
Americans than any other prison. The prisoners nick-
named it the Hanoi Hilton after the American hotel
chain. The camp had walls that were 15 to 20 feet (4.5 to
6 meters) high, topped with broken glass and barbed wire.
Soldiers guarded it with machine guns.

Inside were rooms where the North Vietnamese questioned and tortured the American prisoners. The questioning began soon after the POWs arrived. The American military trained them to offer only their name, rank, birth date, and service number. However, the North Vietnamese wanted information about weapons, aircraft, and bombing plans. The guards would sometimes force prisoners to sit on stools for 10 days without baths, food, or even sleep, to get answers. Then the torture got worse.

The North Vietnamese physically tortured almost every prisoner, even though the Geneva Convention forbade violence. Navy Captain Jeremiah Denton said many North Vietnamese "loathed the torture or simply closed their eyes to it," but others were cruel and showed no mercy. Torturers punched, kicked, and beat the men with rubber straps when they refused to talk. Guards tied the prisoners' arms behind their backs and hung them up for days. This often dislocated their shoulders and almost suffocated them.

During a press conference following his release, former POW Sergeant Michael R. Lenker showed reporters how the guards tied his arms together over his head.

When a prisoner heard a guard's key in his cell door, he knew he was going to be "quizzed" in a torture session. Some sessions could last for hours or days. Guards gave some prisoners electrical shocks. They placed other POWs in holes with biting ants. Sometimes the guards held them under streaming water with their mouths forced open until their lungs were nearly full. Prisoners returned to their cells with broken bones and bloody faces. Sometimes their fellow POWs did not even recognize them.

But the worst torture POWs faced was not physical. It was solitary confinement. Sitting alone in the darkness, unable to talk to his fellow prisoners, a POW could lose hope. Rutledge remembers panicking, desperate to "get out of that ever-shrinking world." Prisoners "escaped" by using their imaginations. Some POWs spent years remembering their childhood. Others practiced an imaginary piano or designed dream houses in their minds.

BREAKING DOWN THE WALLS

The U.S. military tried to prepare its pilots and soldiers in case they became POWs. Most were trained to follow the Code of Conduct. The code outlines what a POW is supposed to do if captured. The main rule is that the prisoner resist his captors constantly.

The code required the POWs to keep fighting like soldiers, even inside the prisons. This meant they had to communicate with each other—something prisoners could be tortured for. However, some would steal pencils or make them out of

CODE OF CONDUCT

For Members of the Armed Forces of the United States

1 I am an American fighting man. I serve in the forces which guard my country and our way of life. I am prepared to give my life in their defense.

2 I will never surrender of my own free will. If in command I will never surrender my men while they still have the means to resist.

3 If I am captured I will continue to resist by all means available. I will make every effort to escape and aid others to escape. I will accept neither parole nor special favors from the enemy.

4 If I become a prisoner of war, I will keep faith with my fellow prisoners. I will give no information or take part in any action which might be harmful to my comrades. If I am senior, I will take command. If not, I will obey the lawful orders of those appointed over me and will back them up in every way.

5 When questioned, should I become a prisoner of war, I am bound to give only name, rank, service number, and date of birth. I will evade answering further questions to the utmost of my ability. I will make no oral or written statements disloyal to my country and its allies or harmful to their cause.

6 I will never forget that I am an American fighting man, responsible for my actions, and dedicated to the principles which made my country free. I will trust in my God and in the United States of America.

The Code of Conduct has six main points.

bread, soap, and charcoal. They would spend weeks drilling through their cell walls with a toothpaste tube to pass notes on toilet paper.

In 1965, Air Force Captain Carlyle Harris made communication safer for all POWs. He remembered a code he had learned during training. All it required was a prisoner's knuckles. In this code, each letter of the alphabet became a sequence of taps. All new prisoners learned the code so they could "talk" with the others.

Prisoners who were not considered a threat were sometimes allowed to wander throughout the prison and talk to other prisoners.

The prisoners were careful when using the code. One man would watch for guards as his cellmate tapped out a conversation on the wall. A prisoner in the next cell would listen through his drinking cup on the other side. Prisoners later said the prison sounded like it was full of woodpeckers during the guards' afternoon naps.

With these tapped messages, it was as if the POWs had telephones in their cells. The most senior POW at each camp served as the leader and chief communicator. Navy Commander James Stockdale at Hoa Lo, for example, tapped messages that prisoners passed from cell to cell. He also compiled a list of POWs' names and

*Commander James Stockdale
(1923–2005)*

"broadcast" news from new prisoners using the tap code.

These strong leaders also helped enforce the Code of Conduct. Stockdale ordered prisoners to reject offers of "early release" in exchange for helping North Vietnam. He said the POWs' loyalty to each other was the most important thing.

North Vietnam separated these leaders from other POWs. Stockdale and others spent more than four years in solitary confinement. However, the POWs would cough or sweep using the rhythms of their tap language to send messages to the isolated prisoners. Tapping also helped the POWs survive torture. The torture sessions often left a prisoner so wounded and exhausted that he could not get up from his cell floor. Some POWs say that even a joke tapped through their wall gave them hope.

The POWs found ways to feel victorious even while being tortured. The Code of Conduct says a POW should not give up information that could harm his fellow prisoners. However, torture could push anyone to say or do almost anything to stop the pain. So the POWs adapted the code to make it practical. Senior POWs announced that prisoners could give up a small amount of information after they no longer could take the torture. But the prisoners were never supposed to give in to the guards' demands easily. This way, the POWs, working together like an army, felt they were winning the battle.

With these rules, the POWs kept North Vietnam from getting what it wanted most: propaganda. POWs often found ways to resist while appearing to cooper-ate with their captors. For instance, they agreed to write

A South Vietnamese propaganda poster showed a Viet Cong woman and child killing a U.S. soldier.

letters home praising their treatment, then included secret codes that suggested the opposite. The guards also forced the POWs to read communist propaganda over loud speakers to the other prisoners. To further depress the prisoners, the North Vietnamese made the POWs read news reports about the United States losing the war and about antiwar protests in the United States. Yet the POWs fought back by deliberately mispronouncing words and using comic accents.

The torture of POWs reached its peak in 1968. At this time, the American public's support of the war was fading. North Vietnam tried to make the war even more unpopular in the United States. They tortured POWs for refusing to sign "confessions" in which they asked forgiveness for attacking Vietnam. Again, senior POWs like Denton told the POWs how to resist while escaping severe injury. He told them, "Take torture and before you lose your sanity, write something harmless and ludicrous."

Other propaganda attempts were also unsuccessful.

The North Vietnamese forced Denton to appear on television in May 1966. During the program, he blinked the letters "T-O-R-T-U-R-E" in Morse code. U.S. intelligence officers saw his message, and the world learned about the POWs' mistreatment. In July 1966, North Vietnamese guards led POWs on the "Hanoi March" through the

Handcuffed in pairs, 52 prisoners were forced to take part in the Hanoi March.

city streets to raise support for the war. Instead, the world watched in horror as angry Vietnamese people punched and struck the prisoners.

The North Vietnamese later staged films at a camp called Plantation to show the world they were treating the POWs humanely. In the films, the POWs walked through clean halls, played basketball, and even decorated a Christmas tree. However, the world had already seen signs that North Vietnam was not telling the whole story.

HELP FROM HOME

In the United States, the families of those pilots and soldiers the government had classified as "missing in action," or MIA, did not know if their men were in prison or dead. In June 1969, James Stockdale's wife, Sybil, and others formed the National League of Families of American Prisoners and Missing in Southeast Asia. The group thought the United States should pressure North Vietnam to follow the Geneva Convention. Eugene McDaniel's wife, Dorothy, hoped that "public pressure would open Hanoi's

Members of the League of Families of American Prisoners and Missing in Southeast Asia provided support to one another.

29

prison doors wide enough to get a glimpse of what was going on."

League members wrote newspaper editorials and did television interviews. Some traveled to Paris to meet with Vietnamese negotiators during the 1969 peace talks. Some POWs helped their efforts by accepting early release from North Vietnamese prisons. Though most POWs refused early release, commanding officers ordered others to accept it. Seaman Apprentice Douglas Hegdahl, for example, was ordered to accept his release so he could give the names of other prisoners to their families and U.S. military leaders. Hegdahl had memorized more than 250 names by singing them to the melody of "Old MacDonald Had a Farm."

These efforts were successful. The American public eventually seemed to care as much about the POWs as about the Vietnam War itself. Millions of people wore aluminum bracelets with the names of the MIAs and the dates they went missing.

The U.S. government felt it had to do something to help POWs. In December 1970, the United States made a bold rescue attempt. A U.S. helicopter dropped into the courtyard of the Son Tay prison camp, about 20 miles (32 km) outside Hanoi. U.S. forces quickly killed guards and broke into cells. However, there were no American POWs inside. They had been moved to another camp

A model of the Son Tay prison shows the layout of the camp.

months before. Nonetheless, the failed raid showed North Vietnam that the United States would not abandon the prisoners.

The North Vietnamese also felt they had to act. Communist leader Ho Chi Minh died in 1969. After this, the new North Vietnamese leaders announced that their

Ho Chi Minh (1890–1969)

American prisoners were officially POWs, not war criminals. The brutal torture suddenly ended. Guards removed prisoners from solitary confinement. They gave the POWs more rice and meat and even breakfasts of sugared toast. The prisoners could now write home. Denton welcomed these changes with joy and said, "Night had turned to day!"

LIFE IMPROVES, THEN FREEDOM AT LAST

After the Son Tay raid, the North Vietnamese quickly moved more than 350 POWs to the Hanoi Hilton. This prison was centrally located and easily defended. For years, the prisoners had listened to each other's muffled tapping. Now they were face-to-face. They shook hands and hugged each other. The POWs gave the prison a new nickname: Camp Unity. They declared themselves members of the 4th Allied POW Wing.

Today the Hanoi Hilton is a museum and historical site.

33

This was because Vietnam was the fourth war in which Americans had been POWs.

However, there were soon problems. The men had to sleep so packed together on the floor that they could not even roll over. Fights broke out over small things such as water spilled on someone's sleeping mat. Senior officers struggled to keep order.

The POWs organized "Hanoi University" to occupy themselves. Using their cell floors as chalkboards, prisoners taught classes in everything from languages to auto mechanics. Between classes, they sang in a choir, acted out movies, and played with checkers made of bread.

For years, the United States and North Vietnam could not agree on how to end the war. In July 1972, the U.S. Congress promised to withdraw U.S. troops only after North Vietnam released all the American POWs. That December, the prisoners in Hanoi felt days of intense air raids rattle their cells. These "Christmas bombings" forced the North Vietnamese to return to negotiations. The United

The wing of an American B-52 bomber remained submerged in water near Hanoi nearly 20 years after it fell during the Christmas bombings.

States and North Vietnam finally reached an agreement.

On January 23, 1973, President Richard Nixon announced a cease-fire and the coming release of the POWs. When the prisoners at the Hanoi Hilton heard this news, Navy Lieutenant Gerald Coffee said the men "stood quietly, hardly breathing." Air Force Lieutenant Colonel

Robinson Risner called the men to attention. They saluted, bringing the heels of their rubber sandals together with a sharp slap. Later in the cells, there was laughing, weeping, and confusion.

Before North Vietnam released the first POWs on February 12, 1973, the men received showers, haircuts, pants, matching beige jackets, and black shoes. They were thrilled with simple things such as zippers and shoelaces after years of wearing prison clothing. But the men's emotions bounced between hope and fear as they prepared to leave. They worried about what their families would say to them. Stockdale worried about returning home with hair "now totally white" and feeling "crippled." Some POWs did not believe they were free until they saw the U.S. transport plane on the runway. McDaniel remembered that "as the wheels took off, the cheers shook the plane."

During "Operation Homecoming," 591 known American POWs were flown to Clark Air Base in the

Philippines. There they got to do basic things that felt like luxuries. They called home. They ate all the steak and ice cream they wanted. They soaked in warm baths and slept on soft beds.

Like many POWs, Army Captain Robert T. White was severely underweight at the time of his release.

MOVING ON

When Jeremiah Denton stepped off the plane at Clark Air Base, he spoke like an officer who had just won a battle. "We are honored to have had the opportunity to serve our country under difficult circumstances," he said.

Captain Denton was in the first group of POWs to be released.

Naval flight surgeon Captain Robert Mitchell studied the POWs after their return. He thought loyalty like Denton's was key to the prisoners' survival. Generally, Mitchell found the POWs in better mental health than other veterans. Soldiers who had been on the battlefield in Vietnam had nightmares, and some were depressed for years after they got home. Very few POWs had these problems, and some were even physically healthier.

Mitchell also believed the POWs survived because they were older and better educated than the average soldier. The average POW was 33 years old, had graduated from college, and, as a pilot, had received training to be an officer. The average soldier was 19 years old and had one year of college.

The American public treated the POWs differently from other Vietnam veterans. The POWs were treated like heroes. They got parades, gifts from strangers, and dinner at the White House. Other veterans were often treated with suspicion.

More than 2,000 Americans were still considered

In April 1973, 11 former POWs shared the honor of throwing the first pitch at a Major League Baseball game between the New York Mets and the Philadelphia Phillies.

missing in action when the POWs were released in 1973. Twenty years later, the U.S. Congress declared that, while there may have been living servicemen left behind, none were likely to still be alive. "With those who are missing, there's uncertainty. It's harder to know when to give up hope and when to begin grieving," said Ann Mills Griffiths, executive director of the National League of Families of American Prisoners and Missing in Southeast Asia. Efforts to locate and identify the remains of MIAs continue today.

The former prisoners have found various ways to

share their experiences. Many have written books; others have made films. Some ex-POWs have returned to Vietnam to visit the camps. During a tour of the Hoa Lo prison, Air Force Captain Ronald Bliss said he could still "hear the screams ... because it was—it is—a hard place."

Upon their release, there was concern among the prisoners that they would lose track of each other. The night before flying home from the prison camps, Lieutenant Colonel Bob Craner thought, "Now this group is going to be busted wide open and spread all over the United States." But today, many of the surviving POWs stay connected through reunions, a newsletter called *Free Press*, and the Internet.

Stockdale, one of eight POWs to receive the Medal of Honor, praised this community for its "loyalty to our military ethic, loyalty to our commander in chief, loyalty to each other." Most of the POWs returned proud that they had survived horrifying circumstances with dignity. For many, this remains the clearest U.S. victory in the controversial Vietnam War.

Glossary

editorials—statements that express an opinion in a newspaper or magazine or on the radio or television

humanely—kindly, with mercy

loathed—hated

ludicrous—ridiculous or laughable

Morse code—system of signaling using dots and dashes sent as sound or light

negotiations—discussions in order to come to an agreement

parasites—organisms that live on or in another organism in order to get nourishment or protection

propaganda—information spread to try to influence the thinking of people; often not completely true or fair

shackles—pair of metal cuffs for the wrist or ankle of a prisoner

DID YOU KNOW?

- Many POWs held in the Korean War (1950–1953) gave in to their captors' demands. Morale was low, and more than one-third of the POWs in that war died. In order to avoid these problems in the future, President Dwight D. Eisenhower established the Code of Conduct in 1955.

- Most of the 30 POWs who escaped did so within days or weeks after being captured. They still had the strength to navigate the dangerous jungle. No prisoners escaped from North Vietnam.

- Lieutenant Commander John McCain, later a longtime U.S. senator from Arizona, has spoken of his admiration of fellow POW Mike Christian. Christian sewed an American flag on the inside of his shirt with a bamboo needle and collected bits of string and cloth. After the guards discovered it and he was tortured, he started making a new one.

- In letters from his family, a POW might find that the first letter of each word in a sentence spelled out a message about how the war was progressing.

IMPORTANT DATES

Timeline

1965
American ground troops join the fight in South Vietnam; American pilots begin bombing North Vietnam.

1966
In July, POWs are beaten during the "Hanoi March."

1969
In June, the wives and families of POWs form the National League of Families of American Prisoners and Missing in Southeast Asia; in September, communist leader Ho Chi Minh dies.

1970
In December, the United States attempts to rescue POWs from Son Tay camp.

1972
In July, Congress passes an amendment requiring the release of POWs before U.S. troops are withdrawn from Vietnam; in December, the U.S. military launches the "Christmas bombings" of Hanoi.

1973
In January, President Nixon announces a cease-fire and the release of POWs; in February, Operation Homecoming begins with the return of the first wave of POWs.

IMPORTANT PEOPLE

JEREMIAH DENTON (1924–)

First POW to spend four years in solitary confinement; he alerted the world to the mistreatment of POWs by blinking the word torture *in Morse code on television; he served as a U.S. senator and wrote* When Hell Was in Session; *he is the director of a humanitarian group*

DOUGLAS HEGDAHL (1947?–)

Fell overboard in the South China Sea and became a prisoner of war at age 23; he was ordered to accept early release and returned to the United States in 1969 with information from the camps; he then became a survival school instructor for 30 years

JAMES STOCKDALE (1923–2005)

Major organizer of the resistance movement inside the prison camps; he received the Medal of Honor; he and his wife, Sybil, wrote about the family's war experience in the book In Love and War; *after the war, he taught and served as a college president*

SYBIL STOCKDALE (1924?–)

Helped organize the National League of Families of American Prisoners and Missing in Southeast Asia and promoted the POW cause for which she received the Navy's Distinguished Public Service Award; she was a teacher, James Stockdale's wife, and mother of their four sons

WANT TO KNOW MORE?

More Books to Read

Caputo, Philip. *10,000 Days of Thunder: A History of the Vietnam War.*
New York: Atheneum Books for Young Readers, 2005.

Murray, Stuart. *Vietnam War.* New York: DK Publications, 2005.

Myers, Walter Dean, and Ann Grifalconi. *Patrol: An American Soldier in Vietnam.* New York: HarperCollins, 2001.

Saenger, Diana, and Bradley Steffens. *Life as a POW: The Vietnam War.*
San Diego: Lucent Books, 2001.

Zeinert, Karen. *The Valiant Women of the Vietnam War.* Brookfield, Conn.: Millbrook Press, 2000.

On the Web

For more information on this topic, use FactHound.

1. Go to *www.facthound.com*

2. Type in this book ID: 0756538467

3. Click on the *Fetch It* button.

FactHound will find the best Web sites for you.

On the Road

National Prisoners of War Museum

496 Cemetery Road

Andersonville, GA 31711

229/924-0343

A museum that honors American prisoners of war and shares their experiences; includes a replica of a cell from the Hanoi Hilton

Vietnam War Museum

954 W. Carmen Ave.

Chicago, IL 60640

773/728-6111

Located in the city's "Little Saigon" area, the museum features uniforms and gear from the Vietnam War, including replicas of cages used to hold POWs

Look for more We the People books about this era:

The 19th Amendment

The Berlin Airlift

The Civil Rights Act of 1964

The Draft Lottery

The Dust Bowl

Ellis Island

The Fall of Saigon

GI Joe in World War II

The Great Depression

The Holocaust Museum

The Kent State Shootings

The Korean War

The My Lai Massacre

Navajo Code Talkers

The Negro Leagues

Pearl Harbor

The Persian Gulf War

The San Francisco Earthquake of 1906

Selma's Bloody Sunday

September 11

The Sinking of the USS Indianapolis

The Statue of Liberty

The Tet Offensive

The Titanic

The Tuskegee Airmen

Vietnam Veterans Memorial

A complete list of We the People titles is available on our Web site:
www.compasspointbooks.com

INDEX

About the Author

Danielle Smith-Llera has taught literature, writing, history, and visual arts to students ranging from elementary school to college. She is also a widely exhibited visual artist and plays violin in chamber groups. Danielle earned an undergraduate degree from Harvard University and an MFA degree from Old Dominion University. She lives with her family on the marshy edge of the Chesapeake Bay in Norfolk, Virginia.